B. Chirva, Y. Krasnozhan

SOCCER
Analyzing the game with the professional team players

2016

УДК 796 332
Ч 64

Ч 64 **Chirva B., Krasnozhan Y.** Soccer. Analyzing the game with the professional team players. – Moscow, 2016. – 68 c.

ISBN 978-5-98724-190-5

Considered is the component of professional soccer team theoretical training – analyzing the game with players.

Issues of coaches' organizational and analytical preparation to game analysis and its structure and content are addressed. Recommendations on improving of quality of theoretical classes are given.

The book's materials are designed for coaches working in professional soccer teams and youth soccer.

УДК 796 332
Ч 64

ISBN 978-5-98724-190-5

CONTENTS

INTRODUCTION

Training of players may be considered from different perspectives, and among other things we may mark two components of it: practical and theoretical.

Players' theoretical training may be exercised to a certain extent directly on course of them performing drills or training games, for example by means of certain objectives to players on performing some actions, error correction, explanation of nuances of actions for them in one or another situation etc.

With that, it may be exercised in the pure form also: using special theoretical trainings, including analyzing recent matches.

There are three coaches' approaches developed concerning the frequency of analyzing the game with players:

– some believe that analyzing the game is necessary only in rare cases, generally in extreme situations for the team;

– others are convinced that it is better to hold an analysis of several games at once to identify truly systematic problems in team preparedness to the game;

– third hold to an opinion that every game played by the team should be basically analyzed with the players.

Each of coaches' points of view on the frequency of analyzing the game with players mentioned above is supported by the experience and naturally has a right to exist.

With that, while considering the connection between the frequency of analyzing the game and the professional team sport results, we may note the following.

Professional football is not just a football game, it is football game in the context of some competition. So each competitive game presents another step towards achieving certain final result in competition (taking certain position).

In this regard it appears that having played the match players should definitely know what «gaming step» have they took and how they can perform the following «gaming step» more confidently.

Players may timely get answers to these questions with quite systematic game analysis. It gives ground to say that the approach suggesting the analysis of each played game is more preferential for the professional football.

It has to be noted that regardless of coaches' point of view on frequency of analyzing the game with players they anyhow face a problem how to achieve greater efficiency of these classes.

Possibilities to have greater impact on players with an aim to improve their prowess and team play quality are related to settlement of set of issues on organization and execution of game analysis.

Issues of organizational preparation to game analysis, analytical preparation of coaches, structure and content of game analysis, coaches' behavior and conversation with players in class may be considered as the main.

Taking into account that these issues are considered insufficiently in football methodological literature nowadays, this book attempts to define and discover the most efficient approaches to organization and execution of game analysis with the professional team players.

For this purpose the football experience, groundworks on analyzing the game in other team games, and also recommendations of experts in spatial organization of human intercourse were analyzed.

GLOSSARY

The following terms will be used in this book:

– algorithm – the precise set of instruction, describing the sequence of actions of some performer for achieving the result, some task solution;

– jogging – running (shambling) at an average speed of 2-3 mps, with flopping by relaxed foot and very short phase of flight: once one foot thrusts off the support, the another immediately goes down on the support;

– the attacking zone – pitch are no further than 35 meters from the defending team goal-line;

– the defending zone – pitch are no further than 35 meters from the attacking team goal-line;

– play line – team of players with sufficiently well-defined along the length of the pitch zone of actions in play (defenders, midfielders, wingers and insides, forwards);

– interpretation – explanation of a real situation or ideological position;

– informativeness – a degree of possibility with which we may guess about the description of characteristics, merits and abilities of the tested, and also about his behavior in one or another situation based on the results of a testing;

– orator – from a Latin *oro* – speak;

– proxemics – subsection of social psychology studying spatial and time organization of human intercourse;

– rhetoric (from Greek *rhetorike* – speech craft) – science discipline studying patterns of generation, transition and perception of a good speech and quality text;

– the middle zone – pitch area between the defending and the attacking zones approx. 40 meters long;

– flipchart – magnetic marker board with a clip for a sheet or a block of paper, flipped over as a notebook.

For notes

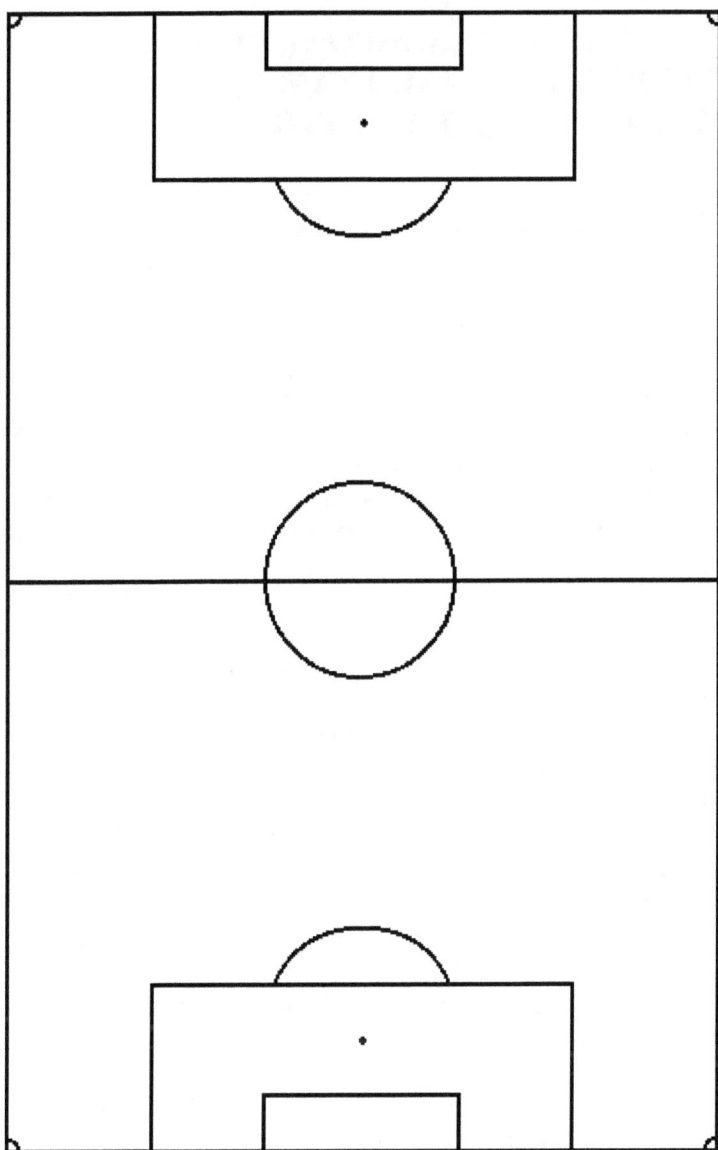

CHAPTER 1.
ANALYZING THE GAME WITH PLAYERS AS A COMPONENT OF PROFESSIONAL TEAM THEORETICAL TRAINING

1. 1. Purposes and main strands of players' theoretical training

Successful functioning of any professional football team suggests the acceptance by players of a certain, one for all procedure of sporting and usual activity.

The range of main issues of functioning of professional football team, on which it is important to have the unity of players, is considerably wide.

Players should come to common understanding in issues on goals the team pursue, the football it's keen to play, how to train, how its living is organized in this regard and in many other things.

Difficulties here are related to the fact that players may be much different in age, experience, prowess and pace of learning ability, length of service in certain club, present different «football schools», be of different nationality.

Inevitably, each of them, and firstly players possessing solid sporting experience, having played in various teams under different managers, has own certain mindset on football in all of its aspects.

In this regard theoretical training plays a significant role in development of a certain, one for all players approach to various issues of its functioning (fig. 1).

Concerning the team play construction players should understand and realize suggested play conception, principles and rules of performance of attacking and defensive actions, tactics in certain play situations.

Fig. 1. Main strands of professional football team theoretical training

Taking into account that play conception and principles determine the content of training process, players should also consistently receive information on planning and tasks of trainings at certain preparation stages, connection between the training work and results of play activity, impact and meaning of certain drills, level of individual preparedness.

The successful team performance is impossible without a display of a winner mentality by players – it is an aspiration of every player to win in game episodes individually, and so education of this play mentality is an important component of theoretical training.

The special section of professional players theoretical training presents the familiarization of players with information revealing pedagogical and medical aspects of their health preservation.

Relevance of this knowledge for players is due to two reasons at least.

Firstly, cases of getting injured occur more often on training rather than in competitive games, and secondly even players with a huge experienced should be protected from performing high-injury actions (random or during drills).

As for the organization of team living, it is necessary that rules of conduct, suggested to players in the context of competitive, training and social activity, are perceived by them, become accustomed and do not cause a negative attitude.

There are possible additional directions in theoretical training as a process of knowledge transfer to players.

Particularly, there are often players in teams, who already ponder on coaching work in the future and so begin to try to understand its specificity. Naturally, these players, showing obvious interest in seeing into characteristics of training process and play construction, should be given particular attention from all the points of view.

In sum, we may note that efficiency of professional players theoretical training grows in case it is performed systematically according to the plan, but also taking into account established realia at the moment.

Theoretical training may be performed by various means: individual, group and team theoretical trainings and conversations, special visual aids, game and training plans, and also by means of game analysis.

1. 2. Analyzing the game with players as a recipe of increasing their prowess and team quality

Regular game analyzing with player is potentially effective recipe of increasing the level of tactical qualification of players and team play quality. This is due to several factors (fig. 2).

Firstly, game analysis may be performed a relatively high number of times a season (around 50-60 times).

```
                    ┌─────────────────┐
                    │  Large amount   │
                    │ of game analyses│
                    └────────▲────────┘
                             │
┌──────────────────────┐     │      ┌─────────────────┐
│ Individualization of │     │      │   Objectivity   │
│  the process of      │     │      │  of presented   │
│ information transfer  │     │      │   information   │
│ and its analysis by   │     │      └────────▲────────┘
│       players         │     │               │
└──────────▲───────────┘     │               │
           │        ┌────────┴────────────────┐
           └────────│ Factors stipulating the │
                    │ importance of game       │
                    │ analyzing                │
           ┌────────└──────────┬──────────────┘
           │                   │
┌──────────▼───────────┐  ┌────▼──────────────┐
│ The potential for     │  │ The possibility   │
│ steady progress of    │  │ to vary values    │
│ the team towards the  │  │ of critical and   │
│ play perfection       │  │ incentive         │
│                       │  │ information       │
└───────────────────────┘  └───────────────────┘
```

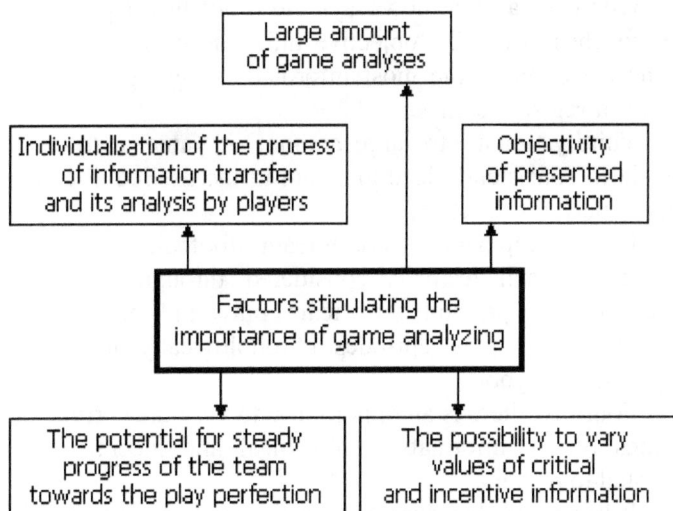

Fig. 2. Main factors stipulating the importance of game analyzing with players for increasing their tactical prowess and team play quality

Nowadays Russian Premier league top teams, for example, may participate in 40 and more competitive games of Russian league and cup and European club competitions throughout the year.

Besides of that, depending on pre-season training system and competition schedule teams gain certain amount of friendly matches (10-15 and more) on course of pre-season, in breaks in competition stages, in certain cycles between games.

Secondly, the information players receive during the game analysis is objective.

Gone are those days when coaches had to analyze the game with players basing only on their visual memory data. Now there is possibility to use, besides game visuals, the statistics on players' technical and tactical and motion activity in games, registered and analyzed by experts not only from the certain club, but also out of club organizations.

One can say that nowadays the problem for professional team coaches is not the objective information obtaining itself, but the selection of the most informative figures from a vast number of registered ones.

Thirdly, thanks to large amount of game analyses it is possible to consistently lead the team in the desired direction in terms of play construction.

For development of certain team «football philosophy» it is better if each team is considered through the lens of conception and principles of team play and not using the interpretation of play episodes chronologically in terms of «played well or poor».

Fourthly, there is an opportunity to vary the correlation of volumes of the information of critical and incentive nature suggested to players.

It happened that during the game analysis considered are various players' mistakes: «didn't run up to here», «gave a wrong pass there», «lost the one-on-one fight here» etc. This is done in order to exclude wrong actions or at least to lower its number, i.e. to improve the play of certain players and the team as a whole.

It should be considered though, that pointing out players' mistakes and faults in play may present the criticism of players in a varying degree not only in terms of their playing activity, but personal qualities and abilities (intelligence, courage, volitional powers, talent).

Obviously, critical analysis of footballers' play is necessary condition for their development, but systematic and massive criticism of players often occurring during poor team performance results in inappropriate psychological background for their prowess perfection.

For example, gamy analysis is impractical with players under 14 y.o. in some European junior schools for this reason.

Certainly, players from professional teams are more mentally stable than young players, but it is important to find an actual balance of criticism and encouraging towards them during the game analysis also.

Fifthly, the process of information transfer and analysis on course of analyzing the game may be personalized with due consideration of players position and their personal characteristics, that would allow to improve quality of data for theoretical training.

The detailed consideration of various nuances of individual and group actions of player of the same position at team meeting often has no practical interest for players of another positions.

In this regard the time given for game analysis may be used more effectively if it is performed in groups of players of the same position and individually in some cases.

Moreover, some players may respond to criticism made in front of the whole team inadequately, perceiving it as degrading, by reason of particular mentality, based on parenting and nationality, status and age. It is preferable to analyze such players' serious mistakes individually.

CHAPTER 2.
ORGANIZATIONAL PREPARATION
TO ANALYZING THE GAME
WITH PLAYERS

2. 1. Defining the time
of analyzing the game
in inter-playing round

The game analysis is not important as such, but as a step on a way of improving the team play quality and achieving victory in the next match. In this regard it is important to define the time of its performing in inter-playing round properly.

It is inappropriate to analyze the game too early or too late relative to its end. This is explained by the following.

In case the game analysis is planned for the very next day after the game, then:

– it hard to assess their and their partners' action precisely for players who didn't recover after the game for such a short time yet, especially after unsuccessful matches;

– the coaching staff that has to link together various impressions on the game, determine issues in team play and ways of its solving, analyze various statistics, has to prepare to the theoretical training amid time shortage and may not get in time to do it in full.

In case the previous game is analyzed with players four or five days after, then:

– to this moment players lose interest to this game that goes down in history regardless of the result, and all thoughts are focused on the oncoming one;

– missed are several trainings on course of which players could have performed completely understanding the feasibility and necessity of performance of suggested drills with due consideration of played game.

Therefore whilst sufficiently lengthy inter-playing round (seven days and more) we may consider the third day after the game before the beginning of the general training of this cycle as the most appropriate time for game analysis. In this case there are more opportunities to solute the identified issues in players' preparedness and play of certain players and the team as a whole and to prepare to the oncoming game better.

2. 2. Preparing the room for the game analysis

The efficiency of theoretical training in any scope of activity and knowledge is higher in case it is performed in the room specially dedicated and equipped for it.

Firstly, various interferences (noises, visual) and discomfort in the room deflect attention and decrease the spirit of exercisers, while the disorder in it urge them to the chaotic reaction and interchange of views.

Secondly, the special technical and occasional equipment allows to present and acquire information better.

All the foregoing fully concerns theoretical trainings in football. Players' interest in game analysis and quality of its performance may vary depending on the room, in which the lesson goes, from the point of its intended function, technical equipment, interior, soundproofing and cleanliness.

The room for the game analysis should preeminently comply in size the number of participants of the lesson. Its optimal area is 35-40 sqm for 20-25 participants. In excessively large room players may become disjointed and go amiss.

Naturally, the room in use should be clean, enlightened, ventilated, with comfort temperature and humidity, without extraneous noise.

Presence of many distracting items (paintings, souvenirs, diplomas, trophies etc.) in the room for the game analysis may relax players attention.

Space allocation for the coach performing the game analysis in the room for the theoretical training has paramount importance.

The «speaker area» should contain a coach's workstation (table and chair), place for the occasional equipment, and also some breathing space.

Various technical and occasional equipment should provide coaches with the possibility to illustrate play situation, tactical idea, theorize and drill both in video and with layout of the football pitch, and with flipchart.

Concerning the coach's position in the room while analyzing the game it may be recommended to turn attention to the following points. It is desirable that:

– there should be no furniture to the left and to the right of the coach;

– there should be no inappropriate items, especially of red colour, distracting players, behind the coach and to the side of him;

– the background the coach is positioned on should be enjoyable for players, the curtain of heavy fabric and deep blue colour is the best for players' attention focusing on the coach.

Nowadays the presence of the room for the game analysis, meeting all the necessary requirements, is not a problem for the top professional football teams. It may occur during the location outside their home stations. In these cases it is necessary to turn attention to the following:

– the room that is planned to be used for the game analysis, should none the less comply the status of certain team;

– it is inappropriate to perform the game analysis in the dressing room.

2. 3. Mounting the layout of the football pitch

For many decades in professional teams and junior schools it is customary to mount the layouts of the football pitch generally horizontal along the length of the pitch (fig. 3).

Fig. 3. Currently conventional mounting of the layout of the football pitch (horizontal along the length of the pitch)

Most probably it is done by analogy with how they dispose chalkboards in schools and other institutions, perhaps since the small space or just because it is easier to mount the layout of the football pitch that way technically.

It has to be noted that while disposing the layout horizontal along the length of the pitch the visual perception of specified game events corresponds with coaches' vision during the game.

This is explained by the following.

In football directions of players' and the ball movements are various, though the general vector of game playing, conditioned upon the shape of the football pitch and the goal position, is from one goal-line to another in parallel with the long axis of the pitch.

In the context of this vector coaches usually positioned at the sideline not far from the point of its intersection with the halfway line visually perceive play moments as to the left or to the right of them, while players – as closer or further from them (fig. 4).

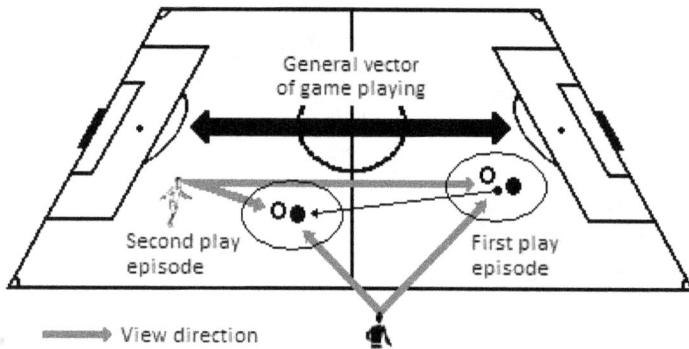

Fig. 4. Visual perception of play moments by coaches and players in the context of the general vector of game playing

Inevitably, mounting of the layout horizontal along the length of the pitch is more useful for the coaches than for the players. In this case players have to rotate this «game image», shown to them at such layout, imaginatively 90 degrees to project it on the pitch.

Indicative in this context are situations when while analyzing the game the coach suggests that player should «come down to the 18-yard box line» or «get up at the player possessing the ball», but at the same time removes the item representing a player or draws the needed player's movement in a horizontal plane.

In sum, the following may be recommended.

It is reasonably to dispose the layouts of the football pitch vertical along the length of the pitch to create the most comfortable conditions for players while analyzing the game for information reception and analysis, and particularly for the compliance in the visual perception of game events on the pitch and demonstrated on the layout (fig. 5).

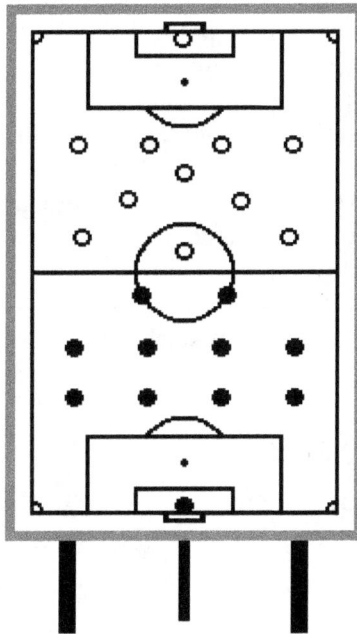

Fig. 5. Mounting the layout of the football pitch (vertical along the length of the pitch) in which there is a compliance in players' visual perception of game events on the pitch and demonstrated on the layout

2. 4. Selecting options of position of those participating in analyzing the game

The efficiency of perception and learning the information presented during the theoretical training largely depends on listeners' positioning in the room relative to each other and the speaker. On one hand it is pointed out by the centuries-long experience of education, and one another – the research data in spatial and time organization of human intercourse (proxemics).

It is completely subject to the players' theoretical training. Usually at such classes players sit down in several rows in front of the coach, which is similar to the classroom-based or theatrical variant of placing (fig. 6).

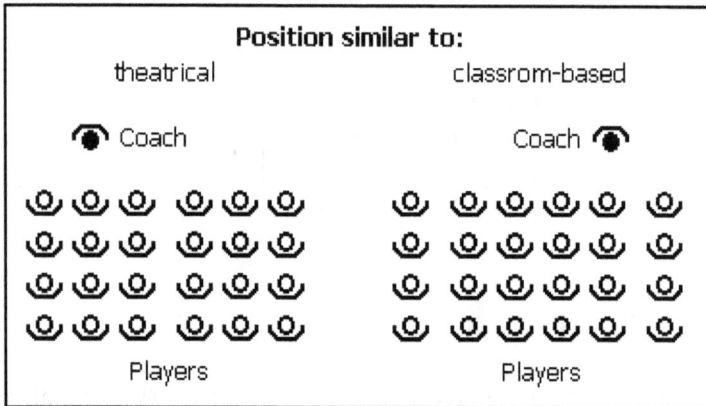

Position similar to:

theatrical   classrom-based

Coach   Coach

Players   Players

Fig. 6. The most common variants of placing of those participating in the professional team game analysis

The coach's principate is secured with such placing of persons. Each of players is «targeted» exactly at him and limited in opportunities to contact partners face to face.

Inevitably, the panel discussion of any issue is greatly hindered: instead of expressing their views to partners, players automatically begin to get in visual and verbal contact with the coach, addressing only to him.

It has to be noted that with the classroom-based and theatrical variants of placing those participating in the game analysis the coach is «point-blank under the gun», especially in case he is standing.

Players' speeches are directed exactly at him, and it is problematic for him to gloss over the direct questions in such circumstances.

Special researches, which assessed the relation between the listeners' position in class during the theoretical trainings and the extent of their interest and learning the received information, have revealed the following.

The zone of the optimal perception and learning the information, shaped like a funnel, is discovered while placing exercisers in several rows one after another. It lies from the center of listeners position to the side seats of the first row and cover all those sitting in the first row (fig. 7).

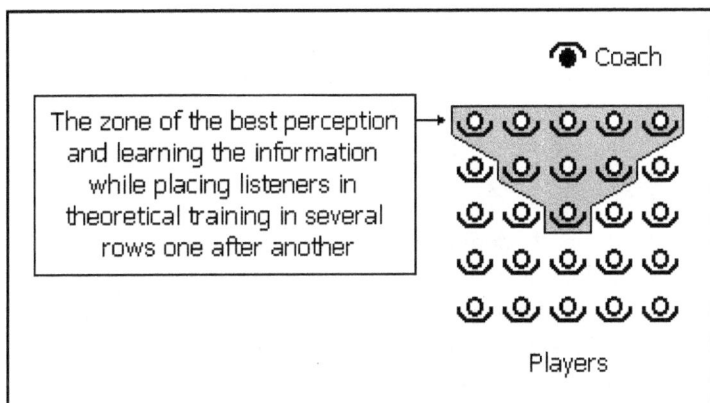

Fig. 7. The zone of the best perception and learning the information while placing listeners in theoretical training in several rows one after another

Those positioned inside this zone, unlike those sitting in the back rows and side seats, are more attentive and active and adopt the received information better.

Interestingly, even those who usually take place in the back row, which are generally hard-boiled listeners, begin to show more interest towards the class in case they get into the zone of the best perception and learning the information.

Basing on above mentioned data, it could be recommended to apply the funnel shape of players' placing during the theoretical training with relatively small number of them (fig. 8).

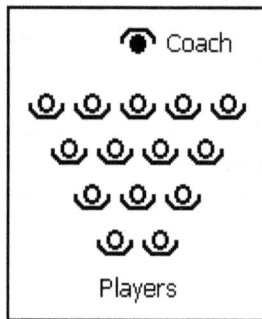

Fig. 8. Placing those participating in professional team game analysis in funnel shape, stipulating worthy perception and learning the information

Sufficiently democratic tone of the lesson is set by placing those participating in the game analysis as horseshoe (fig. 9). In this case all players see each other by sight, each of them may interact with other players, be more unreserved in manner, actively participate in issue discussion, get a hearing from both partners and coach. With that the coach's position and role stay dominant anyway.

With that the atmosphere becomes less formal, players begin to feel themselves full fledged participants of the lesson, their interest towards issues under consideration grows.

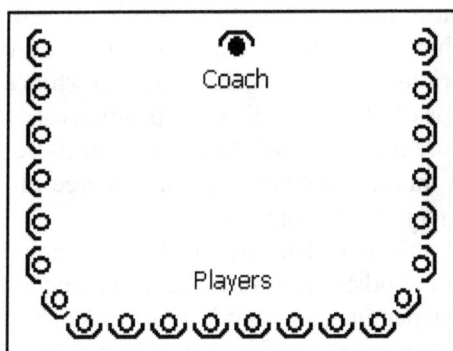

Fig. 9. Placing those participating in professional team game analysis as horseshoe, suggesting sufficiently democratic tone of their interaction

In case those participating in game analysis are situated in a circle (fig. 10), the coach's leading role is not emphasized, although he has all the possibilities to manage the team efficiently.

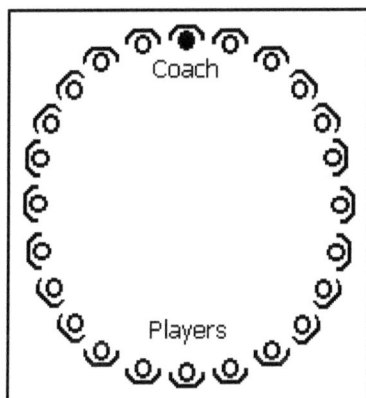

Fig. 10. Placing those participating in professional team game analysis in a circle, suggesting sufficiently democratic tone of their interaction

Circular arrangement in itself instills sense of cohesion in players. In this regard the «round table» is reasonable while discussing serious team play issues, and also while analyzing the game in groups of players of different positions.

Therefore the shape and the position of those participating in theoretical training stipulate a certain degree of democratism and concernment of their interaction.

Taking this into account, while preparing to the game analysis one or another position of the coach and players may be specially set depending on what kind of tasks should be solved during the lesson, on type of lesson (whole team or in groups), psychic atmosphere in team.

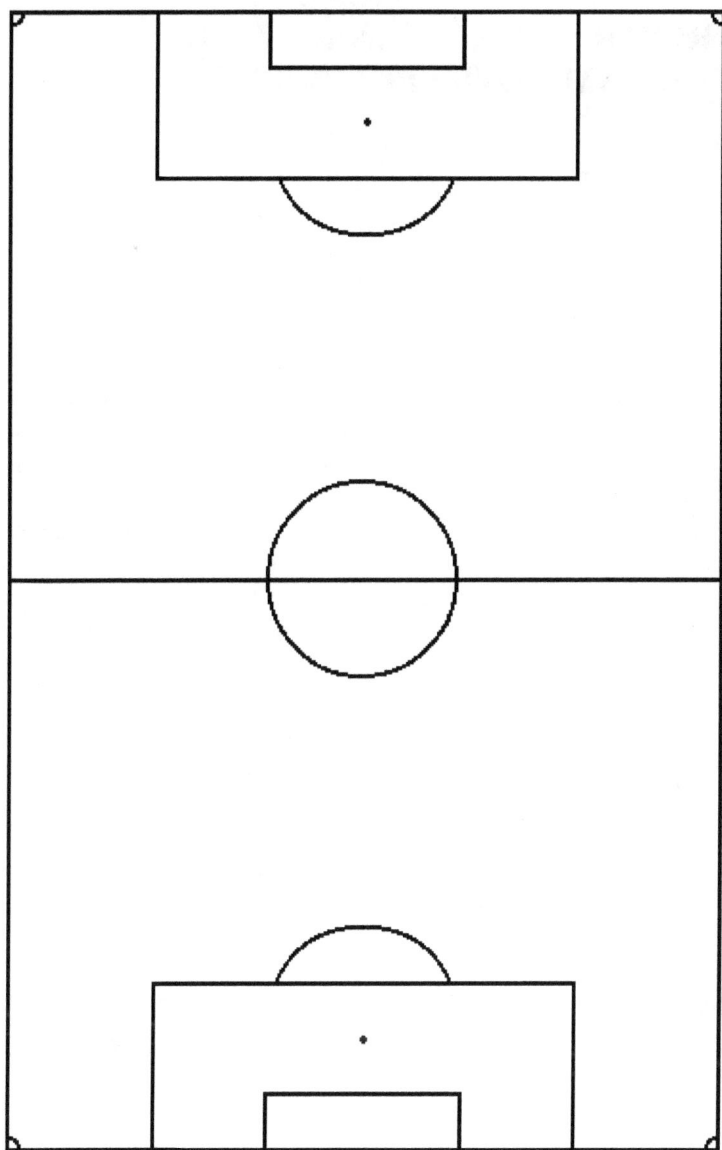

For notes

CHAPTER 3.
COACHES' ANALYTICAL PREPARATION TO ANALYZING THE GAME WITH PLAYERS

3. 1. Main problems coaches facing while preparing to the game analysis

Basically each game analysis with players may be the another starting point on a way of team lay perfection and help towards the victory in the next match and higher result in whole.

For this during the game analysis players should receive a well founded information:

– on team play quality;

– on issues in play and preparedness of team and certain players;

– on ways of solution of identified problems.

While preparing such information it is necessary for the coaching staff to solve five following issues.

First. To define the quality of team play (assess the performance as a whole, in attack and defense, in lines; analyze the success of realization of tactical plan chosen for the match, characteristics of team performance during the game).

Second. To compile an analytical set of play situations with players' group and individual actions, most important in the context of result and observance of the principles of play construction (with a currently optimal balance of situations with correct and incorrect actions).

Third. To specify the problems in team play and preparedness (define system errors in team, group and individual play actions, gaps in preparedness of players and the team as a whole).

Fourth. To enunciate the main strands of training work on solution of defined play problems and gaps in players' preparedness (in the context of the short term and taking into account the fact of the team performing the another competitive match).

Fifth. To prepare to the developments when probably it will be necessary to lift players' spirit, strengthen their confidence in correctness of chosen team play conception, encourage players to hard yet necessary training work (the probability of this is the highest during unsuccessful matches).

Several characteristics may be marked in coaches' analytical preparation to game analysis.

Such preparation suggests work of all coaching staff and experts working in methodological support of team training. As a result of such cooperation manager should have necessary information and clean scheme of its presentation to players, preferably in a relatively short time (up to 30 minutes).

The opportunity of detailed analysis of individual and group actions of players appears in case is planned to analyze the game with groups of players of different positions. In these cases coaches who should perform game analysis with defenders, midfielders and strikers, are naturally destined to change emphasis in their lesson preparation and focus on the analysis of play problems of players of certain position.

While preparing to the game analysis with players, it is important for the coaching staff to analyze all the available information on the game: both internal (from the club experts) and external (from the sources outside the club).

With that the priority has to be placed on objective data, which may both confirm and disprove subjective impressions of actions of certain players and team as a whole. Such data may be captured during the analysis of play situations on video and registration of various figures on players' play activity.

3. 2. Selecting the play situations for its visual presentation for players

There are two possible approaches to the selection of play situations for its visual presentation for players during the game analysis.

One of them come down just to highlighting play situations, necessary for consideration in coaches' opinion, in its chronological order in game, i.e. to creating a game visual reduced several times.

It has to be noted that in these cases both coaches and players have to consequently consider absolutely different play actions and situations during the game analysis.

Another approach to selecting the play situations for its visual presentation for players during the game analysis suggests forming video blocks of play actions of certain trend.

Such work is more laborious, but it is rewarded with better perception of suggested information by players. This is due to the fact that the impact on them is made with alternate volume portions of stuff of specific subject.

This poses the question on subject of play situations or on classification of players' play actions.

Taking into account the essence and rules of football, and also analytical (statistical) patterns of goalscoring in matches of teams of high qualification, we may mark six phases of players' actions in game and subsequently six themes for its analysis:

– the initial phase of actions when the team gains possession (approx. first 5 seconds after taking possession of the ball);

– the major phase of actions when the team gains possession (approx. 5 seconds of possessing the ball);

– the initial phase of actions when the team loses possession (approx. first 5 seconds after losing possession of the ball);

– the major phase of actions when the team loses possession (approx. 5 seconds of being without the ball);

– actions directly while putting the ball into play from set-pieces (while performing free-kicks, corners and penalties, goal-kicks, throw-ins);

– actions during breaks in the game (when the ball is not in play) (fig. 11).

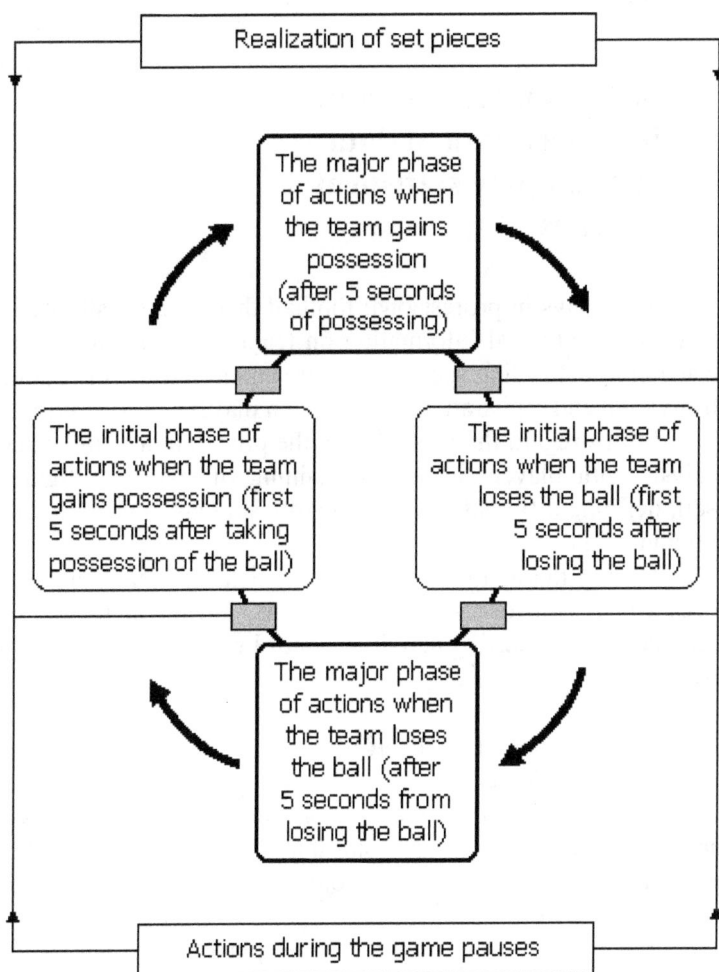

Fig. 11. Phase structure of players' actions in the game

Concerning the technicality of editing video segments of the game we may note that now there is special software not requiring the expensive equipment and special staff recruitment.

Particularly, coaches can make the compilation of match videos by themselves both chronologically and on selected topics quickly and well using their PC and any appropriate software.

3. 3. Characteristics of interpretation of data of team play statistical analysis

Nowadays in professional football there is a possibility to get various statistical information on team play. This data may be acquired both using special software and as a result of routine observation and registration of figures on players' play activity.

In this regard the issue during the preparation to the game analysis with players is not the gaining of statistical figures itself, defining different components of team play, but finding its optimum and correct interpretation.

During the analysis of statistical data of team play it is necessary to consider several provisions, having in mind that methodology of sporting activities control refers to the theory of tests.

What various figures of players' technical and tactical actions may indicate

Some figures of players performing actions with the ball may contain information on result that may be achieved by the team in certain matches and in competition as a whole, i.e. be informative.

Figures of whole team actions of players with the ball in the game, on which the result of the match and whole competition may be predicted with one or another degree of probability, are presented below (see the table).

Figures of whole team technical and tactical actions of players in the game, informative relative to the result of the game and the competition to varying degrees

Figures of whole team technical and tactical actions of players in game	Degree of informativeness relative to the result	
	matches	competitions
Difference between teams in number of actions with the ball with an ultimate output	medium	
Difference between teams in number of play episodes with the ball in opponent's 18-yard box*	medium	
Number of precise passes into opponent's 18-yard box	medium	
Number of actions with the ball performed in the attacking zone (no further than 35 meters from the opponent's goal-line, excluding 18-yard box)	very low	low
Number of actions with the ball with an ultimate output		high
Number of shots on target in opponent's 18-yard box		high
Number of passes inside opponent's 18-yard box		high
Number of play episodes with the ball in opponent's 18-yard box		high

*number of play episodes with the ball in opponent's 18-yard box is the amount of number of performed in 18-yard box shots on target, passes, attempts to outplay, contacts with the ball that didn't result in shot on goal, pass, outplaying

With that much of usually registered figures of players' actions with the ball are not informative relative to the result of certain matches and whole competition and only characterize the playing style of the team and largely depend on game tactics chosen by encountering teams, and course of the game.

Firstly, such figures include generalized quantitative data on various technical and tactical actions performed by the team, specifically:

– time of possession of the ball;
– number of all actions with the ball;
– number of all attacking actions with the ball;
– number of all attacks;
– number of attacks through the middle;
– number of attacks on the flank;
– number of all shots on target with a foot and head;
– number of shots on target from the outside of the 18-yard box (on course of play or from free-kicks);
– number of all passes;
– number of passes of certain distance (on short, medium and long distance);
– number of passes of certain direction (backward, across the pitch and forward);
– number of passes of certain target (preparative, constructive and giving an edge);
– number of movements with the ball;
– number of attempts to outplay;
– number of all defending actions on coming over the ball;
– number of one-on-one's;
– number of interception of the ball;
– number of coming over free ball;
– number of stealing the ball away;

Since mentioned figures of technical and tactical actions of players largely depend on tactics of encountering teams and course of the game it may quite vary from game to game.

How to take figures of efficiency of technical and tactical actions of players in percent

Generally there is so-called efficiency of performing various technical and tactical actions by certain players and whole team in percent, defined for assessment of players' performance. This is done with calculating the ratio of number of some precisely performed actions to total number of these actions, expressed as a percentage.

While using such approach to determination of efficiency of technical and tactical actions of players figures for every player and whole team may be calculated:

– on certain technical and tactical actions;

– on all combined attacking technical and tactical actions;

– on all combined defensive technical and tactical actions;

– on all technical and tactical actions in game.

Moreover, all figures of efficiency in percent of four mentioned groups may be considered for every player and whole team from the perspective of performance of technical and tactical actions:

– on course of the game (in the first and second half, on 15 minutes intervals of the game);

– on place on the pitch (on different halves of the pitch, in certain zones of the pitch marked with some marking or randomly).

Therefore, coaches may have a considerable amount of data at disposal, during the analysis of which the following should be considered.

First. Indeed figures of efficiency of players' technical and tactical actions in percent characterize just a volume of some actions with the ball performed precisely (successfully), of total amount of these actions, i.e. the technicality of performing actions with the ball.

These figures is not reflective of play efficiency of players' actions, i.e. the correctness of their decision-making on performing actions with the ball in one or another game episode.

For example, figures of efficiency of passes in percent don't allow to judge a greater or lesser reasonability of its performance at all.

The actual efficiency of players' actions during the game may be accurately assessed only by coaches, taking into account the tactics chosen for the match, play task received by the certain player, specificity of play situations.

With that figures defining the quality (precision) of players performing various actions with the ball present an auxiliary data and should be considered from the perspective of meaning of certain technical and tactical actions of players in certain zones of the pitch for achieving the necessary result by the team.

Second. The less actions are performed by the player, the more its «value» in percent. For example, in case the player has performed 10 action of certain kind, each of them is treated as 10 per cent, and in case it is 5, then as 20 per cent.

Due to the specificity of football and play position some kinds and variants of technical and tactical actions are performed in matches by certain players a small number of times (less than 10).

In such cases it is inappropriate to conduct a comparison study of figures of actions efficiency in percent of the same player in different games or halves of the match, let alone players of different play positions. This is due to the fact that just one action performed precisely or inaccurately would improve or reduce the efficiency of actions in percent by a large amount.

Put the case the player has performed two passes on a long distance either in the first and the second half of the match. In the first half both passes were accurate, and in the second – just one.

If we compare performance of these passes in the first and second halves fro the perspective of efficiency in percent, it appears that in the first time it was 100 percent, and in the second dropped to 50 percent.

It seemingly gives ground to suggest the breakdown in quality of player's long distance passes in the second time, though in fact he made just one pass less than in the first half.

Therefore, we should consider not the efficiency of actions in percent, but **absolute** figures or performance of these actions (total amount, number of precise and inaccurate actions) during the analysis of technical and tactical actions performed by certain players a small number of times.

With that it is necessary to turn attention to the area of the pitch where certain technical and tactical actions were performed. This is due to the fact that the importance of precisely and inaccurately performed actions towards goalscoring and protecting own goal is heavily varied depending on the zone of its performance on the pitch (zone of losing the ball).

For example, it's one thing if a player trying to outplay the opponent loses the ball in the attacking zone, and another thing altogether when he loses the ball in the defensive zone. This is due to the fact that the possibility of scoring a goal or awarding a penalty during the attacks, beginning from the team coming over the ball in the opponent's defensive zone, is approx. three times higher compared to cases when the team begin such attacks in its defensive zone or in the middle zone of the pitch.

Third. Quite often figures on the efficiency of performance of several combined technical and tactical actions by certain players and whole team in percent are presented while game assessing. Figures of average efficiency in percent may be calculated:
– on all attacking actions;
– on all defensive actions;
– on all actions performed in the game.

If we consider figures of average efficiency in percent of all attacking or defensive actions of certain players, then it is unclear what do they reflect particularly, as either action include totally different technical and tactical techniques.

In order to understand this we should analyze how figures of average efficiency in percent of all attacking or defensive actions of each player are calculated.

The ratio between the number of attacking or defensive actions of each kind, accurately performed by the player, and total number of actions of this kind in percent is calculated at first.

The obtained values are summarized on attacking and defensive actions and then divided into number of kinds of attacking and defensive actions subsequently.

As a result of such «play with numbers» we get figures about which we can say they characterize efficiency of the attacking and defensive actions blends of each player.

As for the efficiency of performance of all technical and tactical actions in play in percent and all the more medium efficiency of actions in whole team play in percent, these figures are almost nonsense, as it is calculated for combined and essentially different (attacking and defensive) kinds of actions.

How to consider figures of players' motor activity

It is customary to register the footage and number of players' movements with and without the ball with different speed while analyzing their play activity.

Precedently the distance and the speed of players' movements were estimated by experts visually on course of matches or using videos of matches. Naturally, significant errors in captured data occurred with such method of registration of motor activity.

Nowadays the motor activity of players in matches may be registered by special automatic measuring system. In these cases all players' movements on the pitch are traced with several TV cameras, and each player is considered as a point in the plane with coordinates X and Y.

After computer processing of data the complex of motor activity figures in play of certain players and the whole team is represented, and usually it is:
– the distance of all movements;
– the distance of moving at a foot-pace (with a speed not higher than 2 mps);
– the distance of jogging and with a subaverage speed (2-4 mps);
– the distance of running with an average speed (4-5,5 mps);
– the distance of running with a high speed (5,5-7 mps);

– the distance of moving with a sprinter run (with a speed higher than 7 mps);

– the maximum speed of movement;

– number of speed-ups;

– the distance of movements on course of the game (in the first and second half, on 15 minutes intervals of the game);

– the distance of all movements on course of the game (in the first and second half, on 15 minutes and 5 minutes intervals of the game);

– the distance of movements with a different speed on course of the game (in the first and second half, on 15 minutes intervals of the game);

– percentage ration of the distance of movements with a different speed.

Seemingly figures on motor activity of players in the game, received with computer technology, are precise and clear, though it's not all that simple. There is a possibility that unfounded inferences may be made with reference to them. To elude this, it is important to consider several points during the interpretation of such data.

First. They often try to compare players of own and opponent's team by the footage of all movements performed in game, and also to gear the result to the whole team figures of movements distance of encountering teams.

During the analysis of data on the distance of certain players' movements as figures of motor preparedness level it is necessary to take into account that individual footage may be largely due to entirely different factors, specifically:

– play position;

– play task;

– the degree of activity of direct opponent from the rival team;

– characteristics of play construction of encountering teams;

– time of the ball being in play that may vary significantly (up to 10 minutes and more).

As for the whole team figures of distance of players' movements, it also could be largely affected by substitutions (their number and time during the game).

Players who have performed all 90 minutes generally have distance of movements in the second half less than in the first. Due to various reasons this lowering may reach 500, 700 meters and even more. This means, for example, two substitutions in the beginning of the second half may, all else being equal, result in increasing of whole team footage at 1-1,5 kilometers compared to cases when there were no substitutions.

Football development trends also should be noted during the interpretation of data on distance of whole team movements of players from encountering teams.

Currently the emphasis in play construction in world's best teams is made on minimization of tactically wrong movements of players, allowing to achieve a winning result with the whole team footage less than the opponent's one.

Second. It is necessary to consider the distance of movements in play of certain players from the perspective of value of performed exercise load and directions of training work taking into account the structure of their motor activity.

It is incorrect to say that one player has covered more and another less, as the considerable part of footage of all players' movements in game (from 30 to 60 percent depending on position) is walking.

Another considerable part of footage of all players' movements in game (from 35 to 50 percent depending on position) is jogging.

The distance of movements in play of different players both walking and jogging may differ by more than 1 kilometer. Therefore there may appear situations when overall footage of one player's movements is bigger than another for 1-1,5 kilometers, though this difference is fully due to performance of movements walking and jogging.

It has to be noted that walking and jogging, performed in aerobic mode of power supply in the context of respiratory and vascular systems, are no less than 75-80 percent of distance of players' movements in game, according to various sources.

On this basis some experts conclude that aerobic capabilities are exactly leading in structure of professional players' motor preparedness.

With that coaches are urged to the interpretation of registration data of players' motor activity in games in certain direction, specifically to that it is necessary to pay particular attention to development of players' aerobic capabilities for increasing the footage of their movements.

Indeed the performance of walking and jogging in games presents no special difficulties for professional players and not limited by their aerobic capabilities at all. This load is recovering in the context of power supply mode, i.e. just a background for players performing movements at a maximum speed, major in football.

Third. To win micro episodes of the game players should act very quickly in most cases. Therefore figures on footage and number of movements performed at a maximum speed are the most important during the analysis of players' motor activity in games.

With that there are problems in acquiring such data and its correct interpretation nowadays, caused by several reasons.

A. In most cases in football quick movements of players are starting speed-ups (acceleration), performed by them all out from a standing start or on course of movement with a lower speed.

Such actions are often characterized as movements at a maximum speed, but that's all wrong. This is explained by the following.

To reach the maximum speed of running player needs some time (to cover some distance), greater or smaller depending on the speed of his movement at the initial moment and value of applied efforts.

Researches with players from Russian Premier League have shown that, for example, while performing starting speed-ups from a standing start they may reach their maximum speed of running having covered around 30 meters.

Therefore, the concept of running with a maximum speed and running performed as quick as possible begin to be equal only after player was able to achieve his maximum speed of running.

Up to this moment there is just broadly burst of running speed, but never the movement with a maximum speed.

As for the footage of players' movements in the game with truly maximum speed, the following should be considered.

Firstly, we can talk about registration of players' movements, performed with a maximum speed in the certain game exactly, and not with a maximum speed which may be demonstrated by one or another player in principle.

The individual maximum possible running speed of players may be discovered during the testing within specific conditions, as there may appear no situations in the game which allow players to reach their maximum speed.

Secondly, providing that movements with truly maximum speed is running with a speed no less than 9 mps, the footage of such movements of top class players is heavily varied depending on position, though it is a rare occasion when it exceeds 100-120 meters).

B. Methods of registration of players' quick movements by means of starting speed-ups, which is nowadays in use with involvement of TV computer measuring systems, stipulates errors in precise definition of such motor actions footage as such. This is explained by the following.

Such measuring systems automatically register the speed of players' movements every moment and calculate the footage of their moving with the speed that stay within one of specific speed ranges. There are five following speed ranges of moving outlined more often:

– not higher than 2 mps (walking);

– from 2 to 4 mps (jogging and running with a subaverage speed);

– from 4 to 5,5 mps (running with an average speed);

– from 5,5 to 7 mps (running with a high speed);

– more than 7 mps (sprinter run).

While performing starting speed-ups all out players may reach maximum or almost maximum speed, but may not reach the speed of running corresponding to the speed range of sprinter running (more than 7 mps) because of small distance of such moving and obstacles from an opponent.

Anyhow certain intervals of starting speed-ups quickly performed by players will be added to the footage of their movements with a subaverage, average and high speed by automatic measuring systems (fig. 12).

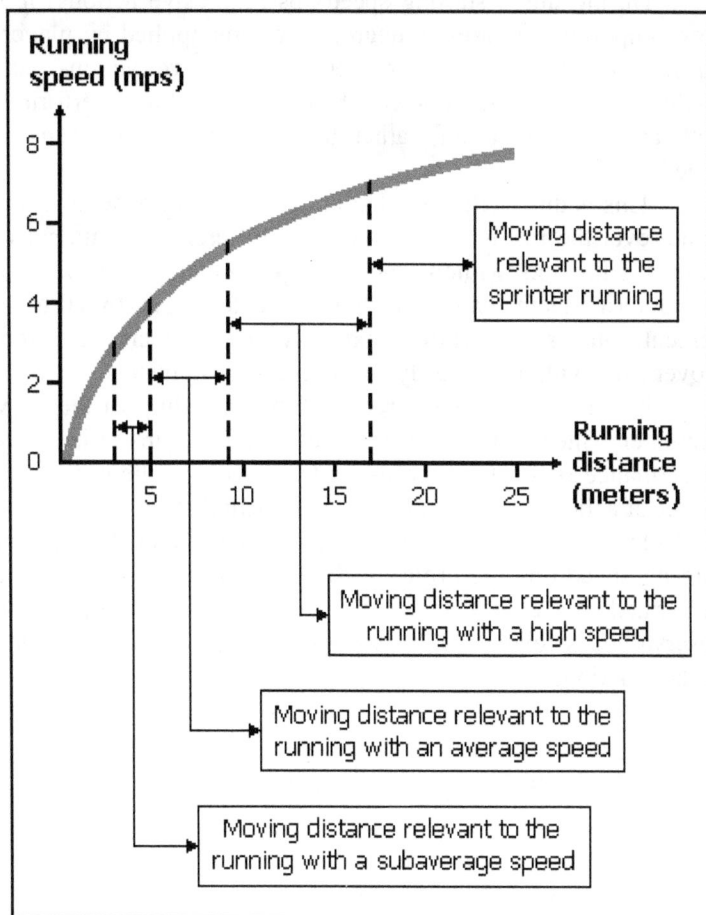

Fig. 12. Example of potential processing of data received during the registration of starting speed-up, performed from a standing start with a maximum speed at 25 meters, by TV computer measuring systems

C. Assessing of players' motor activity in games on footage of moving with a different speed is reasonable in regard to play episodes when speed of players' movement remains at the same level or varies insignificantly for a quite long time (while performing walking or running quite evenly).

During quick starting speed-ups (explosive actions) it is more important to assess a degree of efforts applied by players during the speed-up, i.e. power of explosive actions, and quantify number and footage of staring speed-ups performed with an ultimate output, rather than figures of their running speed.

This is due to the fact that in matches of opponents of the same level the result is determined by difference in number of actions with and without the ball, performed by players of encountering teams exactly with an ultimate output, by 20 to 40 percent, and such actions, naturally, differ markedly from movements with quite steady speed in energy demands.

At present the data received while using various TV computer measuring systems do not characterize the performance of starting speed-ups by players in the context of power of actions demonstrated by them with that.

Therefore the registration of number and footage of starting speed-ups performed with an ultimate out put may be performed by expert coaches given that subjective visual observation is related with inaccuracy during the dimensioning of these actions.

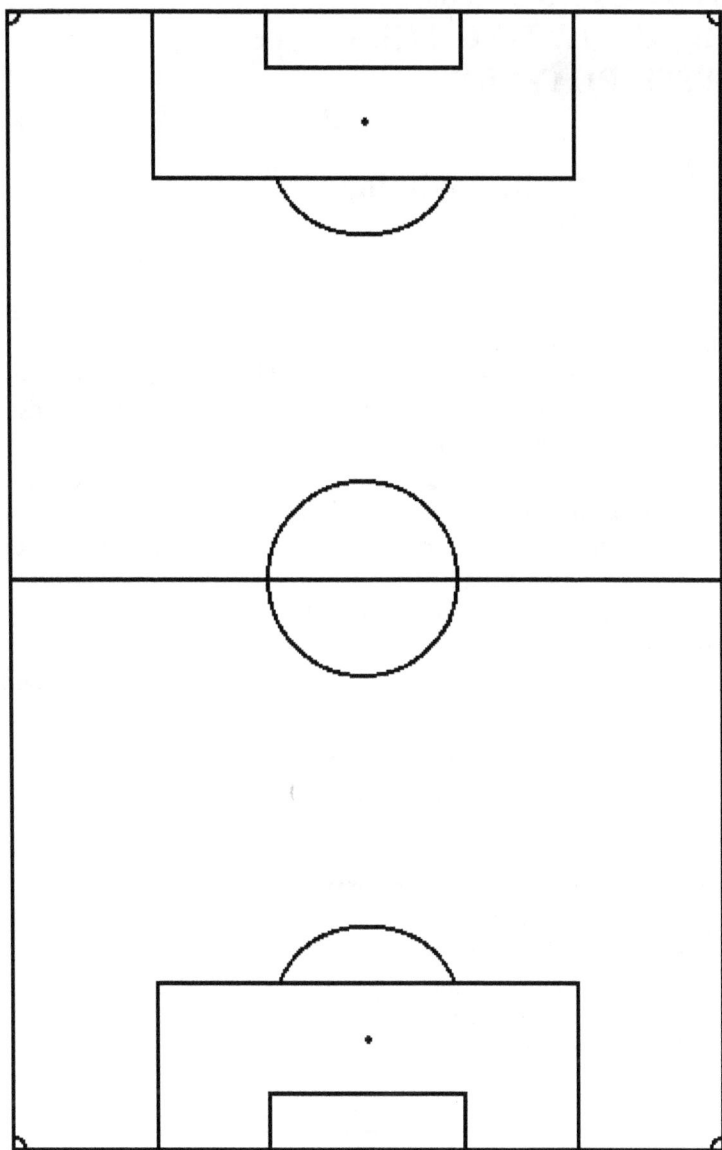

For notes

CHAPTER 4.
STRUCTURE AND CONTENT
OF ANALYZING THE GAME
WITH PLAYERS

4. 1. Game analyzing algorithm

The success of perception of information by players during the game analysis is related to logical sequence of its presentation as well. Such sequence may be observed, if we stick to universal algorithm of theoretical training, which suggests allocation of three parts: opening, main and concluding.

The main part of the game analysis may include three information units in its turn:

a) «the beginning point» – overall assessment of various components of team play;

b) «positives and issues» – the analysis of correct and wrong actions of players;

c) «suggestions» – ways of game problems solving and team preparedness (fig. 13).

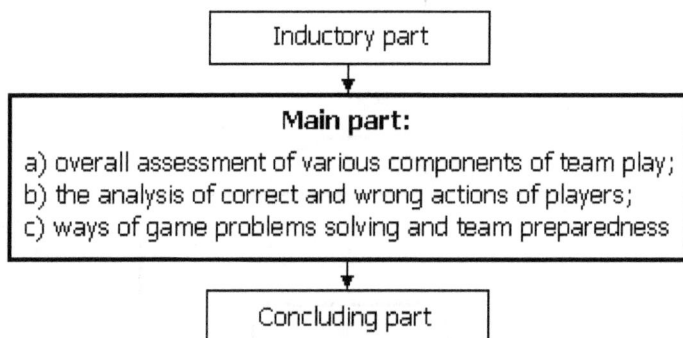

Fig. 13. Algorithm of the game analysis with players

4. 2. Tasks and content of introductory part of analyzing the game

Main problems of introductory part of the game analysis with players are:
– set up a working mood among players;
– acquaint them with an operating mode and problems of this theoretical class.

Sometimes in the beginning of meeting players' attention may be distracted with something. In such cases it is important to help them to put irrelevant thoughts and worries aside and focus exactly on the oncoming game analysis. It is inappropriate to urge players on and use threats and nipping appeals to players' self-esteem for this purpose.

There is an opinion it is necessary to find a spot for a joke or a quirk to create a favorable working environment, in the introductory part of the lesson.

The coach's sally in the beginning of speaking is surely a fine way to attract players' attention, though it is better to begin the lesson in such manner ad hoc and not constantly.

With insufficiently well-planned preparation to game analysis in the context of players' placing in the room front seats (rows) may turn out to be unoccupied. Such players' placing is not the best for successful lesson, so it is preferable to reseat them forward.

With that there may occur problems, as players may take seats in front reluctantly, but it is much better off resolving these problems kiddingly.

In the introduction it is necessary to briefly explain main problems and content of this theoretical training in general, report about its approximate time.

It is important to keep within the announced schedule of the lesson later on, as in this case there will be greater attention of players trusting the coach at following game analysis.

4. 3. Tasks and content of main part of analyzing the game

Tasks of main part of game analysis with players involve:

– analysis of team play and players' individual actions itself;

– informing players about the directions of training work in the short term.

These tasks may be completed with the sequential consideration of three following information units.

First information unit – «the beginning point»

The identical understanding of current circumstances promotes players' interest in game analysis and team unity. Quality data of played game may be used as a reason for such understanding and specific starting point.

In this regard it is reasonable to present the general assessment of various components of team play in the beginning of the main part of game analysis, specifically to characterize:

– the success of realization of tactical plan chosen for the match;

– the attacking and defensive play;

– actions of certain play lines;

– characteristics of game playing by the team at different time intervals;

– psychoemotional characteristics of players' behavior (attitude towards the game, commitment, volitional powers, discipline).

It is best if the assessment of team play quality is based not only on subjective judgments of the coaching staff members, but also on various statistical information of players' play activity.

Second information unit – «positives and issues»

Any player has a certain number of correct and wrong actions in every game. Both kind of actions should be analyzed for players to be able to improve their prowess and the whole team to improve quality of play and achieve better results.

Taking this into account, the emphasis is made on the detailed analysis of correct and wrong players' actions and formalization of main issues in team play and preparedness in the second information unit («positives and issues») of the main part of game analysis.

It is reasonable to give the main consideration to group and individual players' actions that characterize the observance of principles of the attack and defense construction by players most clearly in the following stages of the game:

– in the initial phase of actions when the team gains possession (approx. first 5 seconds after taking possession of the ball);

– in the major phase of actions when the team gains possession (approx. 5 seconds of possessing the ball);

– in the initial phase of actions when the team loses possession (approx. first 5 seconds after losing possession of the ball);

– in the major phase of actions when the team loses possession (approx. 5 seconds of being without the ball);

– directly during putting the ball into play from free-kicks;

– during breaks in the game (when the ball is not in play).

Regardless of how the selection of play situation for visual presentation for players during the game analysis was going on (in chronological order or by subject), we should necessarily analyze scored and conceded goals.

It is important to thoroughly consider not only the goalscoring itself, but also how and where resultative attacks have started up and developed.

It is also necessary to analyze goalscoring chances, created by the whole team and the opponent.

During the analysis of the attacking and defensive play the attention is turned to the «positives and issues»:
– in players' individual actions;
– in interactions of players of certain play lines;
– in interactions of players of different play lines;
The optimal balance of considered play situations with correct and wrong players' actions is defined by coaches in advance on course of the analytical preparation to the game analysis taking into account the current situation in the team.

In conclusion of the second information unit in the main part of the game analysis we should briefly enunciate the main issues in team's play and preparedness (typical mistakes of fundamental nature in group and individual play actions, weaknesses in players' preparedness).

Third information unit – «suggestions»

This information unit in the main part of the game analysis presents a familiarization of players with issues needed to be solved during the preparation to the following match and the main strands of training work during that period.

It is recommended to write the suggestions announced by the coach following the game analysis down on the flipchart or chalkboard. This would help to retain the working attitudes for the oncoming inter-playing round even the most forgetful players.

4. 4. Tasks and content of concluding part of analyzing the game

Even though the concluding part of the game analysis with players is short in time, it is necessary to specially prepare to its conducting also.

Considering the conclusion, we should build on the main subject of the lesson, and it is better to put the conclusion points in writing.

It is necessary to summarize all the considered stuff in the concluding part of the game analysis with players. It is also important to motivate players to the upcoming training work, assure them it will necessary deliver.

The game analysis with players is reasonable to end on a positive note regardless of its result.

4. 5. Methodological recommendations on analyzing the game

Practicing coaches and specialists theorists working in football and other team games advise to abide by several rules during the game analysis.

1. To keep a close eye on the team, turn attention to the players' behavior (their poses and movements), mark those overwrought, silent and unsmiling and encourage them to express their point of view.

2. To suppress players' chattering, though give them an opportunity to take stock of their actions and actions of their partners.

3. To see after the appearance of conversation topics which are beyond the scope of the developed plan of the game analysis and take time to their discussion, to explore the players' extent of interest in considering of this topic and to announce it would be considered later.

4. Not to waste attention on minor issues far from the main strand of the game analysis.

5. To fix the most important matters raised by players on course of the game analysis in mind or on the paper and to expound own view at raised issues in the end of the lesson during the summarizing.

6. Not to get into lengthy argument with players.

7. To use such terminology and intonation that each player understood what was said in a way the coach wants, while analyzing technical and tactical actions.

8. It is better to express criticism towards players in a quiet, friendly tone. Criticism should be obligingly fair on the first hand, and be confirmed with statistical data as far as possible on the second.

Being in possession of registration data on players' technical and tactical actions, the coach may elude the negative attitude towards him, as the objective registered data provide a positive background for discussion of mistakes and way of its solving.

9. To lead players to positive conclusions on course of the game analysis, joining own opinion with players' ones, unless they discord crucially.

10. It is important to prompt players to discuss the status quo and how they would realize the attitudes, received at the game analysis, later by themselves.

For notes

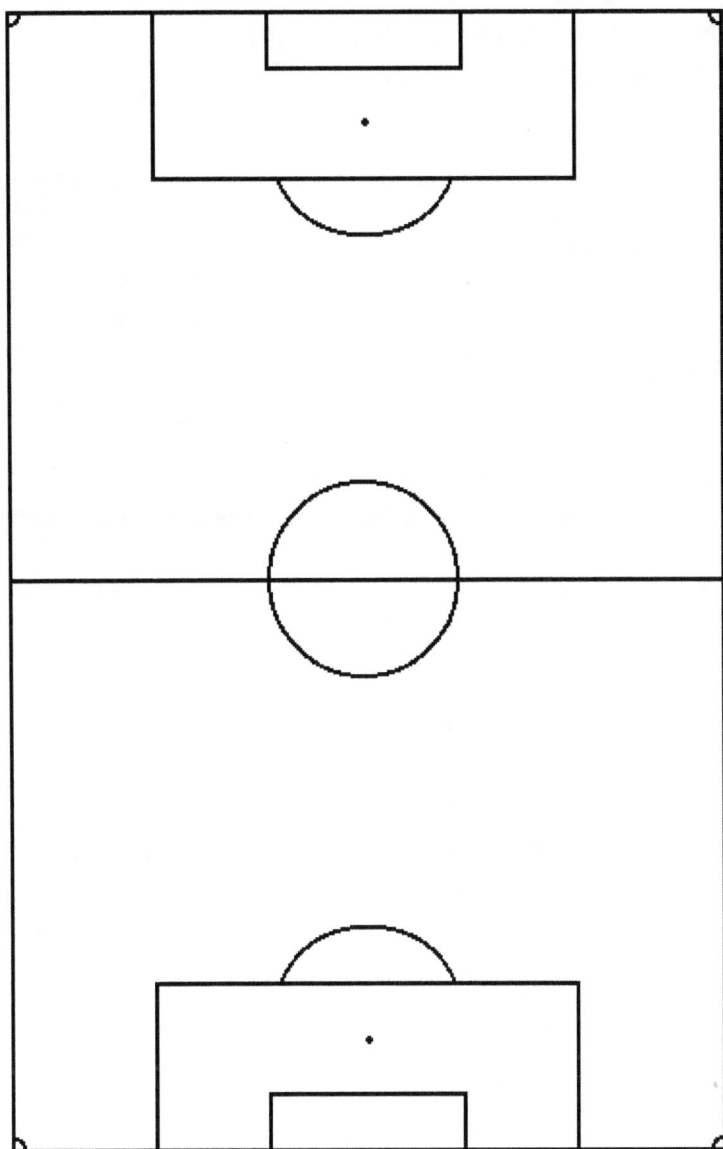

CHAPTER 5.
POSSIBILITIES OF IMPROVING
IN QUALITY OF THE ORETICAL
CLASSES

No matter how long players and coaches are working together, how familiar they are, what kind of relationship they have, the theoretical training, including the team play analysis, suggests neither more nor less than coaches' public speech.

The success of public speaking depends not only on the speaker's knowing of matter in question core, but also on his abilities to convince people, i.e. on his oratory skills.

Oratory largely depends on the speaker's personal qualities (authority or ability to come by himself and bring listeners to the special psychoemotional level).

With that the centuries-long experience and research show that opportunities to convince people during the public speaking may be increased in cases when the speaker follows some certain rules of conduct and conversation.

5. 1. Recommendations
on coach's dress code
and shoes at the
theoretical training

Overwhelmingly the professional teams' theoretical trainings are performed at special own sports centers (training grounds). Such centers (training grounds) are in fact the second home for players and coaches, and naturally the homely atmosphere suggests wearing specific clothes and shoes.

Particularly, players and coaches spend considerable time in such things of sport outfit as shorts and beach slippers while at the training ground. Players generally stick to such dress code and shoes at the game analysis.

In some cases, apparently under the influence of the homely atmosphere of the training ground, coaches also conduct such lessons, wearing shorts and slippers, sometimes without their socks on.

Taking into account the necessity of observing certain status and stressing of the lesson importance by coaches, it seems appropriate if the coaching staff clothing would be stricter than players' by means of sweatpants and sports shoes.

5. 2. Recommendations on coach's behavioral actions at the theoretical training

During the theoretical trainings some coaches, especially with limited experience, may feel difficulties related to how to behave, how to position oneself and move, where to watch, how to assess and maintain players' attention.

This difficulties may be resolved or at least minimized, having considered recommendation of experts on behavioral actions of those public speaking, i.e. coaches, directly conducting the game analysis, presented below.

Recommendations on the coach's behavior before the theoretical training and at its beginning

1. To arrive late without good cause means disrespect for the team, though it is inappropriate to arrive early in the room where the session will be held.

2. The lesson should not start straight off, it's better to look around, get ready (lay out notes, adjust the layout of the football pitch) and give players an opportunity to focus.

3. There is no point to wait for those who linger and draw attention to their appearence after the beginning of the lesson.

4. While beginning the lesson there is no need to show discontent in case there are some technical blunders or some late attendance.

5. It is better to speak opening remarks while standing and being directly in front of players.

Recommendations on the coach's position, movements and motion on course of the theoretical training

1. It is better to speak while standing than sitting, and it is preferable to change position a few steps occasionally on course of speaking (excluding its beginning and conclusion).

2. The walk should be regular and slower than usually.

3. There is no need to turn back on players, weave, keep arms in static position during the movement.

4. It is not allowed to keep hands in pockets.

5. There is no need to twist and turn some minute objects, it is better just to take pointer or marker in hand.

Recommendations on the direction of coach's view on course of the theoretical training

1. It is necessary to look at all players alternately.

2. With scattered location of players in the room it is reasonable to allocate sectors and shift gaze from one sector to another, without overlooking anyone.

3. There is no need to look at the floor, ceiling, window, into space, stare at inappropriate items.

4. While formulating an idea it is appropriate to briefly remove gaze from players, but we should shift gaze back slowly.

5. To try to keep eye contact with players through all the lesson.

Recommendations on the assessment of players attention and interest by the coach on course of the theoretical training

1. The following characteristics of players' behavior point at their attention and interest:

– the sight is directed to the coach;

– body tilted towards the coach, position on the edge of the chair to be closer to the coach;

– head tilted to the side.

2. We may judge players' disregard and discontent by such moments of their behavior:

– the sight is directed to the side;

– lack of ocular movements;

– the neck is straighten, shoulders go up and down, the gaze wanders from side to side;

– hands interlocked tightly;

– the head is supported by the whole hand;

– light stroking of nose and neck;

– tapping with a finger or a foot on something;

– legs stretched forward and crossed, body reclined, head leaned forward.

Recommendations on stimulation of players attention and interest by the coach on course of the theoretical training

The level of players' attention and interest on course of a quite lengthy theoretical training does not remain constant all the time, and so it is necessary to stimulate these psychic processes.

Players' attention and interest during the game analysis may be maintained and increased in the following manner.

1. To make the beginning of speaking interesting, unusual, memorable at the most.

2. To avoid mind-bending statements and droning and use tropology (figures of speech, epithets, comparisons, hyperbolas and sententious sayings).

3. To withdraw from considering the major point (main subject) for a brief spell.

4. To involve special rhetorical tricks of stimulation of listeners' activity:

– a transition from monologue to dialog with players;

– a dead ender with the following searching for the answer in public (raising of questions and objections and its considering) and coming to some conclusion;

– providing a situation causing a question «Why?» for players.

5. To use humor as needed.

Recommendations on lowering the coach's unrest and uncertainty on course of the theoretical training

1. It is important to be familiar with the theme under consideration.

2. To prepare to the lesson carefully and shape a clear plan of its conduction.

3. To address to players most open for information reception in the beginning of speaking.

4. To speak louder than usual, bravely and aggressively.

5. To increase the «wattage» of gestures, poses and body language.

Recommendations on the coach's work with the layout of the football pitch and flipchart on course of the theoretical training

1. With a vertical arrangement of the layout of the football pitch or its designation on the flipchart the upper half is always considered to be the opponent's half, and bottom one – the own team's half.

2. The magnetic items on the layout, simulating players and the ball, should be clearly visible for players on one hand, and on another should not be disproportionately big.

3. While marking the football pitch and its parts on the flipchart it is necessary to strive to observe approximate proportionality of their length and width, determined by rules of football.

4. For marking players' actions of the flipchart we should use common conventions, presented in fig. 14.

5. While direct involvement of hand for demonstration of some moments, events and ideas on the layout or flipchart:

– it is necessary to keep eye contact with players and not to turn back to them for long (and better not at all);

– it is totally prohibited to express a thought with a back exposed to players;

– it is preferable to change position relative to the layout or flipchart (to the left and to the right of it) to pay attention to both halves of audience quite evenly.

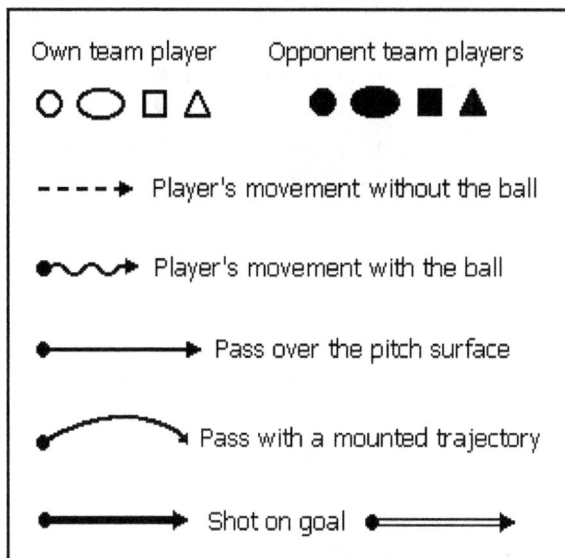

Fig. 14. Common conventions of players' actions

5. 3. Recommendations
on coach's speech culture
at the theoretical training

Any theoretical training suggests convincing players in something, i.e. deliberate and intentional impact on their consciousness, will and feelings. Generally such impact is performed by coaches using spoken language.

Words have to make sense, have a specific goal, lie over players' mind, change their behavior and mindset, to inform players, convince them of something and rouse them to some action.

With that consideration must be given to every word, because even one careless or harsh word may have a negative impact on players, become the reason of strained relations and even conflicts in team.

Therefore the issue of speech culture for the coach profession is surely relevant, it is knowledge of literary standards (spelling-to-sound rules, rules of accentuation, language use, construction of sentences and phrases) and ability to use expressive linguistic means in various communication conditions according to the speech goals and content.

There are several recommendation on composition of spoken language by the coach, suggested for enhancing efficiency of impact on players at the theoretical training.

1. The coach should pour in every word as much power and energy, as possible, and there should be a call to follow the idea felt in his voice. Preference should be given to shorter sentences which are better perceived aurally and memorized.

2. To set generally medium pace of speech (number of words per minute), avoid too long pauses. It is believed that the most optimal tempo of public speech is 120 word per minute.

Significant pause (so called gross pause) is reasonable with the semantic transition, and also in such cases when it is necessary to underline the importance of the last phrase before the pause of the first after it.

3. It is important to find the optimal speech intensity taking into account the size of room, in which the lesson goes, and the distance to players. In case the coach speaks very loud it creates a nervous atmosphere and urges players to behave loudly. Before the announcing of important idea the voice may be lowered and hence force players to concentrate to hear what was said.

4. The intonation should be natural, and it could be changed depending on situation in order to change the players' mood.

5. To use special words and terms, providing the feedback, more often: personal pronouns (I, you, we, you and I), verbs (let's try to understand; please note; please think).

6. To exclude potentially used:
– slang expressions (colloquial and wrong in grammatical form words and expressions);
– filler words;
– words and speech patters adopted from the underworld.

7. To turn attention to the correct setting of accents in certain words.

It should be stressed that perfection of speech culture through realization of noted above and another possible recommendations obligingly suggests speech self-control and systematic analysis of own speakings.

AFTERWORD

The evaluation of one of components of the professional football team theoretical training – the game analysis with players – allows several conclusions on its meaning, tasks, preparation and performance.

First. The game analysis with players is potentially effective recipe of increasing the level of tactical prowess of players and team play quality.

Second. The task for the coaching staff during the game analysis is not only to analyze of previous match and present a project for further work, but also to create atmosphere of interest for players as a necessary condition of their progress.

Third. Quality of the game analysis largely depends on its organizational preparation, specifically the settlement of such questions, as:

– defining the time of the game analysis in certain inter-playing round;

– technical preparation of the room for the lesson, including the «speaker's working area»;

– selecting options of players' and coaches' position at the lesson, with that the most favorable conditions for solution of planned tasks of the game analysis are provided.

Fourth. Coaches' analytical preparation to the game analysis allows to present the information:

– on team play quality;

– on issues in play and preparedness of team and certain players;

– on ways of solution of identified problems.

During the analysis of internal (from club experts) and external (from the sources outside the club) information the priority has to be placed on objective data, which may both confirm and disprove subjective impressions of actions of certain players and team as a whole.

Fifth. The structure of the game analysis with players includes opening, main and concluding parts.

The main part of the gamy analysis may consist of three information units:

a) «the beginning point» – overall assessment of various components of team play;

b) «positives and issues» – the analysis of correct and wrong actions of players;

c) «suggestions» – ways of game problems solving and team preparedness.

Sixth. The success of impact on players at the theoretical training depends not only on the coaches' knowing of matter in question core, but also on abilities to convince people using conversation, i.e. on oratory skills. This prowess largely depends on the coach's personal qualities, including the ability to come by himself and bring listeners to the special psychoemotional level.

Seventh. Opportunities to convince players in something may be increased with coaches observing certain rules of conduct during the game analysis. These rules touch upon their following actions:

– before the lesson and at its beginning;

– position, movements, motion and visual communication with players on course of the lesson;

– assessment and stimulation of players' attention and interest at the lesson;

– elimination of potential difficulties, caused with unrest and uncertainty;

– work with the layout of the football pitch and flipchart.

Eighth. The issue of speech culture for the coach profession is surely relevant, it is knowledge of literary standards and ability to use expressive linguistic means in various communication conditions according to the speech goals and content.

Perfection of speech culture by coaches is possible with implementation of recommendations on composition of spoken language, its self-control and systematic analysis of own speakings.

BIBLIOGRAPHY

Альтман С., Трутнев В. Программно-технический комплекс «Футбольный тренер» / С. Альтман, В. Трутнев // «Футбол-Профи». – Донецк (Украина). – 2005 (август-сентябрь). – С. 16-21.

Аркадьев Б.А. Тактика футбольной игры / Б.А. Аркадьев. – М.: Физкультура и спорт, 1962. – 168 с.

Большой словарь медицинских терминов / Сост. В.Д. Федотов. – М.: ЗАО Центрполиграф, 2007. – 959 с.

Ван Гаал Л. Тактика – наша козырная карта / Л. Ван Гаал // Еженедельник «Футбол». – 1995. – № 17. – С. 24-25.

Вайцеховский С.М. Книга тренера / С.М. Вайцеховский. – М.: Физкультура и спорт, 1971. – 310 с.

Волчек И. Тренерское мастерство как фактор, определяющий возможности совершенствования игры футбольной команды / И. Волчек // Теория и практика футбола. – 2009. – № 4. – С. 9-11.

Воронова В. Психологическое сопровождение спортивной деятельности в футболе / В. Воронова. – Киев, Научно-метод. (технический) комитет Федерации футбола Украины. – 2001. – 137 с.

Гаджиев Г.М., Годик М.А., Зонин Г.С. Контроль соревновательной деятельности высококвалифицированных футболистов: метод. рекомендации / Г.М. Гаджиев, М.А. Годик, Г.С. Зонин. – М., 1982. – 24 с.

Годик М.А. Физическая подготовка футболистов / М.А. Годик. – М.: Терра-Спорт, Олимпия Пресс, 2006. – 272 с.

Голденко Г.А. Оценка технико-тактического мастерства футболистов в игре / Г.А. Голденко // Теория и практика физ. культуры. – 1984. – № 9. – С. 11-13.

Голомазов С.В., Чирва Б.Г. Футбол. Теоретические основы и методика контроля технического мастерства / С.В. Голомазов, Б.Г. Чирва. – М.: ТВТ Дивизион, 2006. – 80 с.

Голомазов С.В., Чирва Б.Г. Теория и методика футбола. Том 1. Техника игры / С.В. Голомазов, Б.Г. Чирва. – М.: ТВТ Дивизион, 2008. – 476 с.

Гомельский А.Я. Управление командой в баскетболе / А.Я. Гомельский. – М.: Физкультура и спорт, 1985. – 160 с.

Горбунов Г.Д. Психопедагогика спорта / Г.Д. Горбунов. – М.: Физкультура и спорт, 1986. – 208 с.

Жариков Е.С., Шигаев А.С. Психология управления в хоккее / Е.С. Жариков, А.С. Шигаев. – М.: Физкультура и спорт, 1983. – 183 с.

Зонин Г.С. Коэффициент брака / Г.С. Зонин // Еженедельник «Футбол-хоккей». – 1974. – № 1. – С. 6-7.

Искусство подготовки высококлассных футболистов: научно-метод. пособие / Под ред. Н.М. Люкшинова. – 2-е изд., испр., доп. – М.: Советский спорт, ТВТ дивизион, 2006. – 432 с.

Карнеги Д. Как выработать уверенность в себе и влиять на людей, выступая публично / Д. Карнеги. – М.: «Попурри», 2011. – 416 с.

Качалин Г.Д. Тактика футбола / Г.Д. Качалин. – М.: Физкультура и спорт, 1986. – 128 с.

Козловский В.И. Квалиметрическая оценка технико-тактических действий футболистов / В.И. Козловский // Теория и практика физ. культуры. – 1991. – № 10. – С. 38-40.

Корх А.Я. Тренер: деятельность и личность / А.Я. Корх. – М.: Терра-Спорт, 2000. – 118 с.

Костка В. Современный хоккей / В. Костка. – М.: Физкультура и спорт, 1976. – 256 с.

Кочетков А.П. Целостный подход в работе тренера с профессиональной командой по футболу: учебно-метод. пособие для слушателей ВШТ / А.П. Кочетков. – М.: Принт, 2000. – 138 с.

Кочетков А.П. Управление футбольной командой / А.П. Кочетков. – М.: ООО «Астрель»: ООО «Издательство АСТ», 2002. – 192 с.

Лукин Ю.К. Кашичин А.И., Герасименко А.П. Методика оценки тактико-технических действий футболистов в процессе соревнований / Ю.К. Лукин, А.И. Кашичин, А.П. Герасименко // Помехоустойчивость движений спортсмена. – Волгоград, 1981. – С. 75-78.

Михелс Р. Построение команды: путь к успеху / Р. Михелс. – Киев: Центр лицензирования Федерации футбола Украины, 2006. – 224 с.

Морозов Ю.А. Метод регистрации технических действий футболистов во время игры / Ю.А. Морозов // Материалы научно-метод. конференции по физ. воспитанию. – Л., 1967. – С. 90-92.

Пиз А., Пиз Б. Новый язык телодвижений. Расширенная версия / А Пиз, Б. Пиз. – М.: «Эксмо», 2006. – 414 с.

Полишкис М.С., Поволоцкий Ю.А. Показатели коллективных и индивидуальных технико-тактических действий, как критерии оценки качества игры футболистов / М.С. Полишкис, Ю.А. Поволоцкий // Футбол: ежегодник 1986. – М.: Физкультура и спорт, 1986. – С. 46-50.

Пшибыльски В. К оценке технико-тактического мастерства футболистов / В. Пшибыльски // В книге: VII международный научный конгресс «Современный олимпийский спорт и спорт для всех». Том 3. – М.: СпортАкадемПресс, 2003. – С. 123-124.

Рымашевский Г.А. Управление командой в соревнованиях по футболу / Г.А. Рымашевский // Проблемы спорта высших достижений и подготовки спортивного резерва: материалы научно-практ. конференции. – Минск, 1993. – С. 70-74.

Самборский А.Г. Эргометрические показатели максимальной анаэробной мощности и скоростных качеств у футболистов Премьер-лиги Чемпионата России / А.Г. Самборский // Теория и методика футбола. – 2009. – № 1. – С. 8-11.

Седов Ю.С., Невмянов А.М. Игровая активность в объективных оценках / Ю.С. Седов, А.М. Невмянов // Еженедельник «Футбол-Хоккей». – 1978. – № 23. – С. 6-7.

Соломонко В.В. Тренировка вратаря в футболе / В.В. Соломонко. – Киев: Здоровья, 1986. – 124 с.

Спортивная метрология: учебник для ин-тов физ. культуры / Под ред. В.М. Зациорского. – М.: Физкультура и спорт, 1982. – 250 с.

Стернин И.А. Практическая риторика / И.А. Стернин. – М.: Издательский центр «Академия», 2008. – 272 с.

Тренерское наследие / Сост. А.А. Горбунов. – М.: Физкультура и спорт, 1990. – 335 с.

Туманян Г., Харацидис С. Профессия – тренер / Г. Туманян, С. Харацидис // Теория и практика физ. культуры. – 1998. – № 1. – С. 28-29.

Тюленьков С.Ю. Теоретико-методические подходы к системе управления подготовкой футболистов высокой квалификации / С.Ю. Тюленьков. – М.: Физическая культура, 2007. – 352 с.

Управление командой в процессе соревнований / В книге: Баскетбол: учебник для ин-тов физ. культуры. – М.: Физкультура и спорт, 1976. – С. 229-234.

Фролова М.И. Психолого-педагогические основы руководства спортивной командой: метод. разработка по спецкурсу для студентов ИФК / М.И. Фролова. – М.: РИО ГЦОЛИФК, 1980. – 16 с.

Футбол: учебник для ин-тов физ. культуры / Под ред. М.С. Полишкиса и В.А. Выжгина. – М.: Физкультура, образование и наука, 1999. – 253 с.

Ханин Ю.Л. Психология общения в спорте / Ю.Л. Ханин. – М.: Физкультура и спорт, 1980. – 206 с.

Чирва Б.Г. Аналитические закономерности игры в футбол как основа для выбора тактики игры и построения технико-тактической подготовки квалифицированных футболистов / Б.Г. Чирва // Теория и практика физической культуры. – 2006. – № 7. – С. 28-29.

Чирва Б.Г., Красножан Ю.А. Футбол. Подготовка и проведение разбора игр с футболистами: метод. разработки для тренеров. Выпуск 39 / Б.Г. Чирва, Ю.А. Красножан. – М., РГУФКСМиТ, 2012. – 44 с.

Чирва Б.Г. Футбол. Концепция технической и тактической подготовки футболистов. – 2-е изд., перераб. и доп. 39 / Б.Г. Чирва. – М.: ТВТ Дивизион, 2015. – 352 с.

Якушин М.И. Вечная тайна футбола / М.И Якушин. – М.: Физкультура и спорт, 1988. – 224 с.

www.ingramcontent.com/pod-product-compliance
Lightning Source LLC
Chambersburg PA
CBHW060714030426
42337CB00017B/2868